Original title:
The Purpose of Life: Maybe It's Cake

Copyright © 2025 Creative Arts Management OÜ
All rights reserved.

Author: Evan Hawthorne
ISBN HARDBACK: 978-1-80566-139-9
ISBN PAPERBACK: 978-1-80566-434-5

Baking Together in Life's Kitchen

Stirring laughter in a bowl,
A pinch of joy, that's our goal.
Flour dreams float in the air,
Sugar sweetens every care.

Eggs of chance, they break with glee,
Baking fails? Just add some spree.
Whisking woes into our fate,
Life is better served on a plate.

Joy Without the Calories

Sprinkles dance on cheerful treats,
Calories hide while laughter beats.
Slice of pie? Just take a whiff,
Life's too sweet; enjoy the riff.

Cakes of laughter, frosting of smiles,
Counting giggles, not the miles.
Dessert dreams served on a stand,
Bites of joy from a playful hand.

Cake as Metaphor for Living

Life's a mix of scents and styles,
Chocolate layers bring us smiles.
Whipped cream waves, let's dive right in,
Every slice a chance to grin.

Sprinkle hopes on top with flair,
Cherries plucked from joy's sweet air.
Bake your troubles, let them rise,
In this kitchen, love won't die.

The Lingering Smell of Cinnamon

Cinnamon whispers from the pan,
A spicy tale of 'yes we can.'
Rise and shine, let's make it sweet,
Every moment, a treat to meet.

Sifted dreams in powdered snow,
Life's a recipe, let it flow.
Take a whiff, take a bite,
Every day, we find delight.

Sweet Cadences of Existence

With sprinkles bright, we dance and sway,
In frosting clouds, we laugh and play.
Each cupcake brings a giggle sweet,
As joy becomes our tasty treat.

Life's a layer, thick and wide,
A slice of bliss, we cannot hide.
With every bite, our worries fade,
In sugary moments, memories made.

Frosted Realities and Marzipan Dreams

We float on clouds of sugar bliss,
In cherry-topped fantasies, we kiss.
Marzipan castles, oh what a sight,
Our dreams are baked in laughter bright.

Frosted truths on plates do lay,
With sprinkles of joy in every way.
When life gets tough, just take a slice,
In cakes, we find our paradise.

Nourishment Beyond the Plate

Cupcakes tumble, joy does spill,
A chocolate river, a sugar thrill.
Each muffin holds a secret cheer,
In frosted tales, we persevere.

Pie crust crumbles, life's sweet mess,
A slice of fun, we must confess.
Take a fork, and dig right in,
In bites of laughter, we all win.

Layers of Love and Life

In cakes of comfort, we find our way,
With laughter frosting every day.
Beneath the layers, sweet surprises hide,
In each forkful, joy does abide.

A tart for tears, a cream for cheer,
Life's bakery holds what we hold dear.
So grab a slice, and toast to fun,
In every crumb, we're never done.

Baker's Dozen of Life Lessons

Grab a slice, take a bite,
Life's too short for a diet.
Whip your dreams, don't be shy,
Frosting makes everything fly.

Mix up joy with a dash of fun,
Life's a cake, come have some.
Sprinkle laughter, don't delay,
We're baking hope for every day.

Whisking Together Meaning and Flour

Stir the bowl with gentle care,
Life's ingredients, everywhere.
Add some sugar for a smile,
Bake it warm, let's stay awhile.

Fold in kindness, spices too,
Serving love in every chew.
Spray of joy, a pinch of play,
Whisk it good, keep gloom at bay.

An Ode to Sweet Simplicity

Life is sweet, a slice so fine,
Good friendships shared, a glass of wine.
No complex recipes to try,
Just sprinkles and laughter, oh my!

Light as air, like whipped cream fluff,
Simple things, never too tough.
A cupcake thought, a muffin cheer,
In the sweetness, we persevere.

The Cake of Contentment

A slice of peace, a layer of cheer,
Baked with dreams, we hold dear.
Enjoy the crumbs, savor each taste,
Life is rich, there's no waste.

Cake of joy, frosting of grace,
Every bite is a warm embrace.
With sprinkles of hope, it's our fate,
Dig in deep, don't hesitate.

Life's Rich Ingredients

In a bowl of dreams and flour,
We mix our hopes for hours.
A dash of fun, a sprinkle bright,
A recipe shared in pure delight.

With sugar smiles and buttered cheer,
We whisk away our doubts and fear.
Each layer stacked, a story told,
In every slice, life's joys unfold.

Whipped Whims and Wanderings

A journey through a cake-filled land,
With frosting rivers, oh so grand.
They say to wander and explore,
And taste each slice, who could want more?

With every flavor, laughter's born,
From chocolate hills to cupcakes adorned.
Whipped cream dreams float in the air,
Life's sweet surprises are everywhere!

Baking Memories

Mixing chaos with a pinch of fun,
In every crack, our joys are spun.
From birthday candles, whispers sweet,
To kitchen boogies and dancing feet.

Frosted times, we laugh and play,
As batter fights then finds its way.
The oven hums a joyful tune,
While friendships bake beneath the moon.

Finding Joy in Every Bite

Life's a buffet, oh what a spread,
With cupcakes calling, "Come and be fed!"
Each bite savored, a moment to hold,
In vanilla dreams, our stories unfold.

So take a fork and dig right in,
Let happiness and giggles begin.
For in this slice, we dance and play,
Finding joy in the yummiest way!

A Slice of Gratitude and Glee

In the pantry, treasures lie,
Frosted dreams that flutter by.
Sprinkles dance in morning sun,
Gratitude for all that's fun.

Whisking worries, baking cheer,
Flour clouds when friends are near.
Every bite a joyful cheer,
Glee served up with laughter here.

Icing on the Cake of Being

Life's a cupcake, sweet delight,
With icing swirls, oh what a sight!
Layers of joy and fumbles too,
Savor each moment, me and you.

Sprinkles scatter, laughter flies,
In this kitchen, no goodbyes.
Mixing dreams with frosted schemes,
Every slice ignites our themes.

The Sweetness of Togetherness

Baking buddies, rolling dough,
Silly hats in the kitchen show.
Tasty laughter fills the air,
Sharing slices, showing care.

Friendship layers, rich and grand,
Holding hands while we bake and stand.
Each frosting swirl a memory,
Sweetness, oh, what bliss to see!

Cake Cravings and Cosmic Adventures

Galactic cupcakes, stars on top,
Zipping through flavors, never stop.
Cosmic crumbs in every bite,
Adventure waits in every light.

Floating frosting on the moon,
Cake cravings sing a joyful tune.
Let's take a slice and share the thrill,
In this universe, there's room to fill.

Happy Endings Topped with Icing

Life's a slice, served warm and bright,
With frosting dreams that take to flight.
A chocolate chip, an almond rush,
In every crumb, there's joy to flush.

We mix our laughs with sprinkles rare,
In sugary moments, we shed our care.
Whipped cream smiles and cherry cheer,
Bite-sized memories we hold dear.

Baker's Wisdom in a Vanilla Swirl

With flour dust, we make our stand,
Laughter kneaded by the hand.
A pinch of fun, a scoop of play,
Makes every moment bright as day.

In ovens warm, our dreams take rise,
Sweet vanilla fills the skies.
Taste the joy, let worries flee,
Life's better served with pastry glee.

The Sweetness of Being

Life's a banquet, not a race,
Each bite savored, each sugary grace.
Giddy crumbs on the table spread,
Nourish the heart, to laughter fed.

In frosting so rich, we find our spark,
Dancing with joy, igniting the dark.
Every layer, a story told,
In sugary laughter, we find our gold.

Flour-Dusted Philosophies

Flour on hands, we concoct our tales,
Dreams rise high on our derby sails.
With sugar-coated wisdom in tow,
We giggle through life, let our spirit flow.

Life is icing on a cupcake bright,
Taste it slowly, savor the light.
In kitchens where recipes intertwine,
We learn to feast and brightly shine.

Celebration of Sweetness

In the oven, dreams arise,
Frosting clouds, a sweet surprise.
With a slice, we all partake,
Life's too short, so let's eat cake.

Whipped cream mountains, sprinkles galore,
Each bite's a laugh, who could ask for more?
Baking joy, no need to fake,
Forget your troubles, just eat cake.

Gather 'round, it's time to cheer,
Chocolate bliss, we have no fear.
A happy heart, the joy we make,
With every crumb, we celebrate cake.

So raise a fork, let's have a toast,
To sugary delights we love the most,
Here's to laughter, for goodness' sake,
Let's fill our lives with lots of cake.

A Tasty Reflection

In the pantry, secrets hide,
Sugar dreams, let's take a ride.
Flour storms, a whisk in hand,
Mixing joy, it's truly grand.

A slice of pie, a cookie cheer,
Who'd have thought? The end is near.
But wait! Oh no, just one more bake,
Life is sweet, so let's make cake.

Creamy frosting, swirls that shine,
Every layer, simply divine.
Betray the frown, for goodness' sake,
Dive into happiness? Just eat cake.

Life's a banquet, take your share,
Let's bake laughter, everywhere.
When in doubt, smile and partake,
Happiness awaits—just eat cake.

Recipe for Happiness

Take a pinch of silliness,
Mix with joy, it's pure bliss.
Add a dash of laughter, too,
Then bake it all, just me and you.

Cherry tops on fluffy highs,
Whipped delight that never lies.
Serving smiles with every quake,
Stirring thrills, the world's a cake.

Bake it bright, ignite the fun,
Every slice, we're never done.
In this kitchen, make no mistake,
Life is sweet when you eat cake.

So grab a fork; let's take a slice,
With every crumb, indulge, think twice.
When life gets rough, do what it takes,
Eat it up! Enjoy the cake.

The Sugar Rush Epiphany

Dashing in with sugar high,
Cream-filled dreams that touch the sky.
With every nibble, giggles break,
Who needs a frown? Just eat cake.

Frosted visions, a joyful spree,
Life's a pastry, come and see.
Maple syrup, oh what a shake,
Skip the sadness, let's eat cake.

Life's too short for diet plans,
Grab a fork; take a stand!
Follow your heart, make no mistake,
Chase the happiness—just eat cake.

A sweet illusion or so it seems,
In this world of sugary dreams.
When life gets tricky, take a brake,
Laugh it off, and eat some cake.

Sweet Inspirations

In the oven, dreams will rise,
Sprinkled smiles, sugary highs.
Frosted hopes on every plate,
Life is sweeter when we celebrate.

With each bite, a giggle grows,
Chocolate rivers, whipped cream flows.
A cherry on top, so divine,
Finding joy in every line.

A Slice of Existence

Life's a cake, let's take a slice,
Laughter baked in, just feels nice.
Layers stacked with silly dreams,
Frosted laughter, bursting seams.

Grab a fork, it's time to share,
Friendship served with icing flair.
In every crumb, a memory,
Sugar-coated jubilee.

Whispers of Flour and Frosting

Whisking thoughts with sweet delight,
Flour whispers, oh what a sight!
Piping bags hold secrets neat,
Sweets remind us life's a treat.

Mixing joy with every stir,
Licking spoons, oh what a blur!
Baking memories, warm and bright,
Savoring each sugary bite.

Crumbs of Contentment

In the crumbs, we find our cheer,
Every bite brings friends so near.
Sugar highs and laughter wide,
Tastes of joy, we cannot hide.

Cakes and cupcakes, swirling fun,
Life's a party, come and run!
Sprinkles scattered, joy unfolds,
Crumbs of happiness are gold.

Layers of Wonder

Beneath the frosting lies a tale,
Of tastes and textures, sweet and pale.
With every slice, a giggle springs,
Life's greatest joy is all the things!

Layered high, a tower of cheer,
With chocolate rivers flowing near.
A sprinkle here, a dash of fun,
Who knew that joy could taste like sun?

Cake believes in pure delight,
A dance of flavors, oh what a sight!
A candle's light, we sing aloud,
In laughter's arms, we're ever proud.

A slice of whimsy, served with grace,
Each bite's a journey, a happy chase.
So gather round, bring plates and forks,
For life's a party—let's eat with storks!

Sprinkles of Serendipity

In a world of frosting, all aglow,
Sprinkles tumble, just like snow.
Each color bright, a happy cheer,
A reason to laugh and hold dear.

Flavors collide, a crazy swirl,
Life's little quirks make the heart whirl.
Like jelly beans that dance and roll,
Embrace the chaos that feeds the soul!

Oh, sugary moments, never contrived,
In the mess of joy, we truly thrived.
A scoop of humor, a pinch of flair,
Cake in hand—no worries, just care.

So let's find joy where the sprinkles fall,
In every crack, life's ice cream ball.
With laughter served upon the plate,
Who knew that silliness could taste great?

The Recipe of Being

Combine a smile with a dash of glee,
Add in the laughter, as sweet as can be.
Fold in the chaos, sprinkle it right,
Whisk dreams together, and take flight.

A scoop of kindness, a slab of cheer,
Blend in some shimmer, it's all so clear.
Bake it gently, let passions rise,
Life's sweetest creation is no surprise.

In the oven of moments, warm and true,
Out comes the magic, for me and you.
Slice it up generous, share with a friend,
The recipe's simple—it never can end!

With icing dripped down, like dreams unspun,
Life is a banquet, let's have some fun.
So let's whip up joy, one layer at a time,
For the secret ingredient is simply the rhyme!

Frosted Dreams

In the land of pastries, dreams take flight,
A frosted wonder, shiny and bright.
Cupcakes twirling with every bite,
In this sweet kingdom, all feels right.

Whipped cream clouds float in the air,
Sundaes smile without a care.
Chocolate rivers, oh what a scene!
Life's greatest treasure—more than it seems!

With cherry hats and sprinkles galore,
Let's celebrate life, who could want more?
A buffet of giggles, icing on top,
In this tasty world, we'll never stop!

So raise your forks, and enjoy the ride,
Through frosted valleys, let's take pride.
In this wild journey, we find our song,
For in every dessert, we all belong!

Life Baked in Joy

In a world full of flour, we rise like the yeast,
Finding joy in the whisk, oh what a feast!
With sprinkles of laughter, we decorate dreams,
Life's sweeter with frosting, or so it seems.

We mix up our troubles like batter so thick,
A pinch of good humor, a dash of a trick.
When life throws a pie, we just take a slice,
With cherries on top, oh, isn't it nice?

So gather 'round friends, let's bake up delight,
With giggles and crumbs, we shine oh so bright.
Each layer we build, a story so grand,
Life served on a platter, by our own hands.

Sugar Coated Journeys

Take a trip on a cookie, the icing's so sweet,
Over mountains of marzipan, we skip on our feet.
With gumdrop companions, our laughter cascades,
Adventure is sprinkled like sugar in spades.

We'll hop on a cupcake, to clouds made of cream,
Each bite holds a secret, like a whimsical dream.
Through forests of licorice and rivers of soda,
Life's an amusement, a grand foodie quota!

So roll with the punch, don't worry or fret,
The journey's as tasty as the best cupcake yet.
With memories baked, and friendships aligned,
In this sugar-coated journey, true joy we will find.

Taste the Moments

Every moment we savor, a crumb on our plate,
A pie filled with laughter, let's feast, let's celebrate!
We nibble on tickles and chew on our dreams,
Life's a candy shop bursting at the seams.

With frosting on fingers, we dance in delight,
As cupcakes and giggles take flight in the night.
So let's not be shy, let's dig into life,
Each taste is a memory, a break from the strife.

So grab your forks ready, let's dig in with glee,
For life served together is sweeter, you see.
Each flavor a story, each bite holds a cheer,
In the feast of existence, let's savor it dear.

A Confectioner's Guide

Roll out the dough, our day's recipe,
With laughter as sugar, and fun as the key.
A whisk and a smile, we combine with flair,
In the oven of life, we'll bake without care.

Now sprinkle on joy, and let's frost with charm,
Each challenge we face, just brings us more warm.
With cookie cutter dreams, we shape what we share,
In this confectioner's guide, we'll bake up the air.

So gather your friends, let's whip up some fun,
Life's a cake of creation, and we're never done.
With layers of kindness, and laughter so wide,
In this sweet, tasty journey, we take life in stride.

Citrus Zest and Life's Twists

Life's a lemon, zest and bright,
Squeeze the joy, hold it tight.
Throw in some sugar, make it sweet,
Turn cloudy blues into a treat.

Twists and turns, a rolling pin,
Flour the doubts, let joy begin.
Whip up some laughter in every bite,
Dough rises high, reaching new height.

Baking Love into Every Moment

Mixing joy in a bowl of fun,
Eggs and laughter, we will run.
Butter it up with a generous spread,
Life's a recipe, carefully read.

Sprinkle kindness, a pinch of cheer,
Let's bake memories, year by year.
Summer heat or winter chill,
A cupcake smile can cure any ill.

Sweet Realizations in Flaky Crusts

In flaky crusts, wisdom lies,
Layered dreams under sunny skies.
Roll out the troubles, knead the stress,
Slice through life, don't settle for less.

Cherry filling or chocolate bliss,
Every bite is a tasty kiss.
Life, like pie, has its share of cracks,
But it's the filling that keeps us intact.

Pastry Philosophies

Whisk away sorrows, rise above,
In the oven, there's always love.
Doughy questions, flaky replies,
Bake with laughter, no goodbyes.

Cinnamon dreams and buttered pride,
Let's roll together, side by side.
Puff pastry thoughts, flaky and light,
Life's best moments, a delicious bite.

Sugar Highs and Subtle Lows

In the oven, dreams arise,
Flour flying, sparks of surprise.
Sugar rush and laughter blend,
Life is sweet, around each bend.

With icing thick and fondant light,
We navigate the cake-filled night.
A bite of joy, a dash of fun,
In this world, who needs a pun?

With sprinkles scattered everywhere,
We slice through life without a care.
Frosting dreams swirl high and wide,
In every layer, giggles reside.

So let us bake with hearts so bold,
A side of silly stories told.
For sugar highs and subtle lows,
Are just the way that laughter grows.

A Slice of Existence

Life's a cake that's sweet and round,
With each slice joy can be found.
Layers piled, both thick and thin,
With sugary smiles, we all dig in.

A cherry on top, a wish at play,
We savor moments, come what may.
Each crumb tells tales we can replay,
As frosting drips in a funky way.

We gather round for bites and cheers,
Laughter echoes across the years.
Whisking dreams, we'll take the chance,
With every bite, life's a dance!

So raise your fork, let's share the fun,
With each new cake, our hearts are spun.
A slice of life, oh sweet delight,
In this kitchen, all feels right.

Buttercream Musings on Gratitude

Buttercream clouds that softly swirl,
Whisking up thoughts that gently twirl.
What do we owe to frosting dreams?
Sometimes life's sweeter than it seems.

A spatula dance with joyful grace,
Each recipe a warm embrace.
We savor features in every bite,
Gratitude frosted, oh what a sight!

A crumbly corner, a happy sigh,
In icing whispers, our spirits fly.
So raise your pastry, toast the dawn,
In cake we find where fears are gone.

With sprinkles of joy, we all unite,
Baking happiness feels so right.
In buttercream dreams, we find our fate,
Expressing thanks, we celebrate!

Cake Battles and Life's Meandering Paths

In the kitchen, chaos reigns,
Flour fights and confectioner's stains.
Rolling pins become our swords,
As we joust with cake, and laugh in hordes.

Each fork a weapon, oh what a sight,
We conquer cake with sweet delight.
Fights for the last piece make us grin,
In this battleground, we all win.

Whipped cream on helmets, jelly-filled foes,
Life's meandering paths, where laughter flows.
Through frosting rivers, we sail away,
Finding bliss in cake every day.

So gather 'round for battles sweet,
In our cake saga, we won't retreat.
For life is a party, with joys to seek,
With every slice, our hearts will speak.

Essence of Sweetness Unveiled

In a world that's large and wide,
We find our joy in treats to bide.
Chocolate laughter, frosting smiles,
Life's great riddle, in a pastry style.

Sprinkles dance like little stars,
Whispers of sugar, joy is ours.
Bake a laugh, a pie of cheer,
Eat it quick, before it's here!

Confections of the Heart

My heart's a cake, fluffy and round,
With layers of giggles, it's love unbound.
Marzipan whispers, icing so sweet,
In this bakery life, oh what a treat!

Baking friendships with each warm slice,
Glazed with kindness, it feels so nice.
Sprinkling joy on every meal,
Life's a party, come have a feel!

Sugary Philosophies and Fondant Dreams

What's the secret? It's simple, you see,
Sugar and laughter set the mind free.
A dollop of joy, a pinch of fun,
Together we rise, 'til the day is done.

Fondant dreams wrap us in glee,
A slice of happiness, just you and me.
Let's share a cupcake, giggle and chew,
In this sweet world, it's me and you!

Cravings for Connection

In a bowl of friendship, mix it all up,
A sprinkle of love in every cup.
Slice through the moments, enjoy every bite,
Together we shine, oh what a sight!

Carrot cake talks, red velvet fun,
Each bite we share makes us one.
So grab a fork, and take a seat,
In this sweet life, we're truly complete!

Colors of Joy in Edible Layers

Layers of frosting, a vibrant delight,
Sprinkles like stars, oh what a sight!
Each bite a laugh, a giggle in cream,
In this sweet world, we dare to dream.

Chocolate whispers secrets so bold,
Vanilla hugs warmth, never too cold.
Red velvet dances with passion so bright,
In sugary moments, we find pure light.

Sifting Through Life's Ingredients

A pinch of chaos, a dash of cheer,
Mix in some laughter, for the best of the year.
Flour flies high, like dreams in the air,
When things get messy, we giggle and share.

Eggs crack open, hopes start to rise,
Baking our troubles into edible pies.
With sugar and spice, we create a new plan,
Life's sweeter when shared; every woman and man.

Tart Lessons from the Oven

In the oven's warmth, magic unfolds,
Tarts tell tales of adventures untold.
Some layers are flaky, some just a dream,
But every mishap adds to the cream.

A twist of the lemon, a wink of the lime,
Making mistakes is part of the rhyme.
Taste buds unite, laughter follows the bake,
Even the burnt bits are better than fake.

Flour Power and Sweet Soirees

Whisking up joy, we gather with friends,
A soiree of sweets, where laughter transcends.
Flour on faces, we start the parade,
In this wild kitchen, memories are made.

Muffins that rise with a burst of delight,
Carrot cakes dancing, oh what a sight!
With each tasty morsel, we savor the cheer,
In a world full of cake, there's nothing to fear.

A Taste of Insatiable Wonder

In every slice, joy finds its way,
Sugar and laughter make the day.
Sprinkles of dreams dance on the plate,
Life's sweetest moments can't wait.

Baking adventures, oh what a thrill,
Mixing up wonders, our hearts they fill.
Each bite a giggle, a crumb of delight,
Why be solemn when cake takes flight?

Flour flying high like a whimsical kite,
Eggs on the counter, oh what a sight!
Laughter and icing, the perfect blend,
Who knew sweet layers could be a friend?

So grab a fork, and don't be shy,
In this merry feast, let spirits fly.
With forks and tales, we'll savor the cheer,
For in every moment, life's a sweet sphere.

Frosted Moments of Clarity

With frosting thick, clarity shines,
A sprinkle of truth in sugary lines.
Layers of laughter, fondant so bright,
Slice into happiness, take a big bite.

Tickled by frosting, happiness nigh,
In buttery layers, we let out a sigh.
Life's little secrets tucked in the bake,
Finding joy in each frosted flake.

Between bites we ponder, what do we seek?
Is it the joy, or just cake on our cheek?
Sweet wisdom served on a platter so grand,
Is it frosting, or just the way we planned?

As laughter erupts from a well-iced treat,
Let's eat for joy, life is bittersweet.
A cakeful of moments, bright and absurd,
Unsnap the silence with every sweet word.

Whipped Cream and Golden Epiphanies

Whipped cream dreams flutter and swirl,
In each little dollop, life starts to unfurl.
Golden epiphanies dance on the tongue,
Who knew the smoothness could make us feel young?

Spoons and giggles, what a fine match,
Scooping up happiness, we can't outpatch.
It's an endless buffet of silly delights,
Where laughter and cake take glorious flights.

Sprinkled toppings, with no hint of shame,
Each bite a reminder, we're all in this game.
With creamy concoctions, wisdom we spoon,
Beneath the bright sun or a laughing moon.

So grab a seat at this whimsical feast,
In laughter and sweetness, we're all just released.
With fervor, we savor this hilarious craze,
In the realm of desserts, life's a sugary maze.

Tiers of Meaning and Moments

In tiers of meaning, we stack our joy,
With a frosting smile, let's buoy and enjoy.
Chocolate layers where secrets are held,
What wisdom unfolds when the cake is shelled?

Laughter erupts with each sugary bite,
It's about the journey, not just the height.
From candles to crumbs, we share and we cheer,
In this cake-filled cosmos, we conquer our fear.

Slice by slice, we deepen our creed,
Find significance in each gooey bead.
With plates full of wonder and forks in hand,
Celebrate moments, as sweet as they stand.

So take a big breath, let sweetness unfold,
In layers of laughter, brightly bold.
With cake all around, let's raise our voices,
In this comical dance, life simply rejoices.

Cake Walks on the Path of Wisdom

On the road of sweet delight,
We balance frosting, light as air.
With every step, a crumb takes flight,
Life's flavors blend in joyful flair.

Walking past the bits of doubt,
We giggle at the silly frown.
A slice of joy, that's what it's about,
In every forkful, laughter's crown.

With layers thick, the lessons rise,
Some chocolate dreams, a pinch of fun.
As we unveil our grand surprise,
Life's quirky cake is never done.

Sprinkles of Resilience

Every sprinkle tells a tale,
Of bouncing back when times are tough.
A dash of joy in every pale,
Sweetness makes the rough stuff soft.

When life throws pies and whipped-up cream,
We wear our aprons proud and neat.
With giggles shared, we'll bake a dream,
In batter thick, our hearts will beat.

Resilience rolls in cookie dough,
It rises high, then sometimes flops.
But laughter's here, so let it flow,
We chop and bake, no need for props.

Adversity Layered with Frosting

When troubles stack like crumbling cake,
We spread on frosting thick and sweet.
Each layer hides a laugh to make,
An oven's heat brings us to beat.

The batter's mixed with hope and cheer,
We bake our way through struggles grand.
With spatulas, we have no fear,
A pinch of fun is always planned.

Adversity's a tricky treat,
We slice it thin, then share the fun.
With cupcakes made, we can't be beat,
A sprinkle's gift, our lives undone.

A Symphony of Sugar and Spice

In melodies of sweet and spice,
We dance around with joy on plates.
A symphony that tastes so nice,
Life's laughter bakes, it never waits.

We mix the flavors, blend them right,
A chorus made from all things sweet.
With every bite, our spirits light,
In sugary dreams, we feel complete.

As cupcakes rise, let voices sing,
Harmony within each bite.
With frosted dreams, let laughter cling,
A life of sweets is pure delight.

Flour Power of Existence

Whisk your doubts, let them fly,
Add some sugar, dream high.
In the oven, warmth awaits,
Life's a treat on dessert plates.

Flour dust dances in the air,
Mix it up without a care.
Baking woes may come and go,
But frosting hides the truth, you know.

Batter spills, oh what a sight,
Life is sweeter with a bite.
Sprinkles rain like confetti bright,
In this kitchen, joy ignites.

Slicing cake, let laughter blend,
Each layer brings a brand new trend.
With every fork we find our cheer,
This life is just a tasty sphere.

Joy Served on a Plate

Life's a buffet, grab a slice,
A dash of spice, tastes so nice.
Whipped cream dreams on top we place,
Find your bliss, enjoy the chase.

Laughter mixed with salty tears,
Baked goods calm all of our fears.
Chocolate rivers, icing streams,
In each bite, fulfill our dreams.

Take a fork and dig in deep,
Life's a banquet, no time for sleep.
Every crumb tells a tale,
In this feast, we shall not pale.

So pass the cake, and raise a cheer,
A slice of joy, always near.
Let's toast to moments, oh so sweet,
Life's a treat we all can eat.

The Art of Delicious Living

Measure happiness, add some fun,
Life's a recipe, all can run.
Stir in laughter, don't hold back,
Drizzled joy in every stack.

Rolling pins and playful fights,
Baking dreams to reach new heights.
Flavors mingling, sweet and tart,
Hungry souls, we play our part.

Seek for sprinkles on your day,
Every morsel, come what may.
Layered hopes and laughter spread,
Enjoy the crumbs where dreams are fed.

So bake that cake, and slice it right,
With each piece shared, the world feels bright.
In the kitchen, truth revealed,
Life is best when love is healed.

Craving Meaning

What's the secret? It's no joke,
Layered thoughts, just like a cloak.
Filling hearts with cherry bliss,
In every bite, there's so much bliss.

Crumble worries, bake them out,
Gooey joy is what it's about.
Sprinkle fun with honesty,
Life tastes better, can't you see?

Cupcake dreams, on fluffy clouds,
Laughter ripples, brings in crowds.
Taste the magic, full of zest,
In this cake, we find our quest.

Slice it slow, enjoy the show,
Life's not dull, let laughter flow.
With every piece, discover fame,
In sweet delights, we play the game.

Frosted Dreams and Sugar Cravings

In the oven, magic brews,
Whisking hopes in sugary hues.
Sprinkles dance on a creamy sea,
Slice me up, I want to be free!

Batter spills like my dreams at night,
Flour clouds make the kitchen bright.
A cupcake's smile is pure delight,
In frosting's embrace, all feels right!

With each layer, laughter grows,
Chocolate rivers, sugary flows.
The world is sweet, a glorious trance,
Join the cake, let's take a chance!

Glimpse the joy amidst the crumbs,
In every bite, our laughter hums.
Life's absurd and full of glee,
Cake's the answer, can't you see?

Slices of Joy in a Floury World

In a land where butter meets delight,
We gather round to share a bite.
Cake slices float like fluffy clouds,
Laughter echoes, cheers are loud!

Each forkful bursts with happy cheer,
Crisp edges tease, come and near!
Flour dusters swirl like fairies play,
We're on a sweet adventure today!

Bake your dreams in a tin so bright,
With each scoop, we take a flight.
A dash of whimsy, a pinch of fun,
Life served warm — it's never done!

Let's stack our hopes in a luscious tower,
Frost it thick; let's feel the power.
Cake is life, or so they claim,
With every bite, we play this game!

A Recipe for Happiness

Take a cup of laughter, sprinkle it right,
Mix it with love, and feel the light.
Add a spoonful of jokes, just for fun,
Stir it all up 'til joy has begun!

A dash of sprinkles, colorful and bright,
Whipping up giggles, oh what a sight!
Muffin caps donned like silly crowns,
Baking up memories in doughnut towns!

Pour out the batter in friendship's pan,
Bake it together — the world's our clan.
Slice it with kindness, serve it with cheer,
Each crumb is filled with love, never fear!

Let's whip up a grand confection of glee,
Topped with melting chocolate, just for me.
In our kitchen of life, we'll always strive,
For a recipe of joy that's truly alive!

Celebrations in Every Crumb

Crumbs of joy, scattered wide,
Gather them up, enjoy the ride.
Each little piece, a party found,
In every bite, happiness abound!

Whipped cream clouds float in the air,
Cake slices wink, they truly care.
Sprinkled laughter on this sweet treat,
Turn up the fun, life's truly sweet!

Candles flicker with every wish,
Let's toast to cake, our favorite dish!
Every layer, a story to tell,
In frosting and joy, we all dwell.

So here's to the crumbs, let's not be shy,
Dive into frosting, let laughter fly.
In sugar we trust; it's plain to see,
Life's a celebration, sweet and free!

Dusted Dreams and Life's Cakewalk

In a world of sweet delight,
Sprinkles dance in morning light.
Frosting whispers, giggles bloom,
Baking fortune in the room.

Flour clouds and sugar dust,
Every crumb is filled with trust.
Life's a party, why so grim?
Slice the cake, let laughter brim.

With each layer built on fun,
Creamy dreams for everyone.
Count the candles, eat a piece,
Life's a joke, it's pure release.

So grab a fork, dive right in,
Every slice is where we win.
In this chaos, joy's the aim,
Life's a cake, don't fear the flame.

Layers of Laughter and Cream

A cake stacked high with glee so bright,
Marzipan sun in the pale twilight.
Cherries laugh and giggle too,
Their sweet frosting sings to you.

Jokes baked in every single slice,
Buttercream truth, oh isn't it nice?
Serious faces all around,
Melt away when joy is found.

Sprinkled dreams in icing swirls,
Every moment made for twirls.
Grab your fork and take a bite,
Let's make the mundane feel so right.

Life's a banquet, cakes we share,
Laughter bubbles in the air.
So pick a slice, enjoy the scene,
Join the fun, be light and keen.

Finding Joy in Every Slice

In the oven, hopes arise,
Golden crusts that mesmerize.
Each piece tells a story sweet,
Life is better with a treat.

Have a nibble, take a chance,
Join the silly dancing dance.
With every bite, let giggles flow,
Joy is baked, let it show.

Gather 'round the table wide,
Happiness is a smiling ride.
Whipped cream clouds and sprinkles fly,
Taste the joy, oh me, oh my!

So here's a fork, let's all partake,
In every giggle, life's a cake.
Slice it up and take a chance,
Finding joy in every glance.

Candles for Every Occasion

Candles flicker, dreams ignite,
Every wish takes lofty flight.
Sing a song while we dig in,
To fluff and cream, the joyous grin.

Birthday wishes piled on high,
Silly hats, we laugh and sigh.
Oh! The flavors we adore,
With every bite, we shout for more.

Celebration's gooey core,
Life's a party, who could ask for more?
Light the candles, one—two—three,
Join the fun, come share with me.

Journey sweet through all the years,
Chase away the doubts and fears.
Life's a cake with layers grand,
In every bite, let joy expand.

A Delicate Balance of Butter and Sugar

In a bowl of dreams, we stir and mix,
With butter soft like clouds, and sugar that tricks.
We whisk away worries, fold in some glee,
As flour flies up, just like us, wild and free.

Eggs crack with a pop, as laughter erupts,
A pinch of mischief, where chaos corrupts.
A dash of vanilla, sweet secrets we keep,
This batter of life makes us giggle and leap.

Oven's warmth wraps us, like hugs from a friend,
Each cake a new chapter, a sweet, tasty trend.
When slices are shared, we find joy in our fates,
A delicious reminder: life's never too late.

So let's bake our dreams with a sprinkling flair,
With butter and sugar, please handle with care.
Life's lighter than air, but oh how it bakes,
In this kitchen of joy, there's delight in the shakes.

Revelations in a Rich Ganache

A pot of chocolate, so rich and divine,
It bubbles with secrets, a sweet, gooey sign.
We dip in our spoons, oh what a delight,
Reviving our spirits with each luscious bite.

Ganache like wisdom, smooth on our tongues,
It tells of our journeys, of old songs still sung.
Each layer a story, each drizzle a clue,
In a world made of cocoa, we find something new.

What's life without frosting, a cherry on top?
From trials we rise, so don't ever stop.
When things get too messy, just embrace all the mess,
For laughter in kitchens is life's best success.

So gather your friends and your frosting today,
Let love be the ganache that brightens the way.
With every sweet dare, and every big splash,
We'll stir up our dreams, with a wonderful dash.

The Art of Baking Our Bliss

Rolling out dough, like stretching our dreams,
We sprinkle with laughter — how sweet life seems.
With cookie cutters ready, we shape what we crave,
A masterpiece baked, oh how we all rave!

Whisking our wishes, rise high like a cake,
In this kitchen of chaos, new memories we make.
From oven to table, each bite tells a tale,
Of dreams baked with joy, and love in the mail.

A sprinkle of madness, a drizzle of cheer,
In flour we trust, as we conquer our fear.
From muffins to macaroons, it's all a delight,
In our dessert-filled world, every day feels so right!

So let's dance in the kitchen, flour flies a bit,
With spatulas waving, and laughter — we'll fit.
In every whipped topping and crust that we bake,
We find our true bliss, for sweet happiness' sake.

Joy in Every Sprinkle

A jar of sprinkles, a rainbow so bright,
They dance like our dreams, with pure, playful light.
We shake them with love, atop cakes with a grin,
As laughter and sugar make magic within.

Cupcakes adorned like hats dipped in cheer,
Each bite tells a story, with sweetness so clear.
With icing intentions, we splatter and sprawl,
In this sugary chaos, we're having a ball.

So grab a few friends, let's have our delight,
With layers and laughter, and sprinkles in sight.
For life is too short, let's savor each bite,
In every small moment, let flavors ignite.

Let's fill up our hearts with the joy that we seek,
Through cookies and cakes, our laughter unique.
In this world full of whimsy, we find our own song,
With sweetness and fun, where all of us belong.

The Icing on Our Souls

In the oven of dreams, we rise so bright,
Sprinkles of joy make everything right.
Whipped cream wishes float in the air,
Tasting life's sweetness, without a care.

Baking our hopes, we mix and we blend,
Each slice of laughter, a message we send.
Frosted with love, life's bakery spree,
Gather 'round, friends, come share this glee!

Crumble of worries, we brush them away,
With doughy delights that brighten our day.
Chocolatey giggles, we savor and share,
For every good moment, there's icing to spare.

In a cake of confusion, we find clarity,
With forks as our heroes, we feast happily.
Each bite a reminder of joy that unfolds,
Sweet is the life that each recipe holds.

Delighting in Simple Pleasures

The aroma of cake fills the fun-loving air,
It tickles our noses, without a single care.
Sprinkled with laughter, our hearts take a spin,
In life's tasty kitchen, we always win!

With layers of friendship, we dig and we dive,
Finding that sweetness, we truly feel alive.
A sprinkle of sugar, a dash of the absurd,
In this dance of life, our laughter's the word.

Chocolate chips hug us, they melt in delight,
With every bite savored, the world feels just right.
Throw on some frosting, a swirl and a grin,
Together 'round tables, let the fun times begin!

We're playful bakers on this journey of ours,
Whipping up joy like it's made of the stars.
In the kitchen of life, we whip dreams with flair,
Delighting in moments that make our hearts bare.

Cakes of Carpe Diem

Let's seize the cake, with gusto and glee,
A slice of adventure, come share it with me.
Flour fights flourish, we giggle and play,
Life's sweetest layers beg us to stay.

With toppings of laughter and frosting of fun,
We slice through the chaos, our worries outrun.
Cupcake confetti showers us with light,
Each morsel a moment, our spirits take flight.

In the oven's embrace, our dreams start to twirl,
We whisk up some magic, let it all unfurl.
Grab a fork, my friend, an adventure awaits,
In the cakes of today, we dance with our fate!

Mix in some sprinkles, let happiness bloom,
In a world full of flavors, there's always more room.
A delightful reminder, to savor the day,
With cakes full of joy, we'll laugh all the way.

Savoring Each Layer

Life's a big cake, each layer divine,
We fork through the moments, sip on some wine.
With cherries of mischief and cream whipped with cheer,
We feast on the joys that bring us all near.

The layers of laughter, so rich and so sweet,
With every small nibble, we conquer defeat.
In the pantry of dreams, we bake and we break,
Finding our bliss, one bite at a take.

Candied canopies hold our silly delight,
Each slice full of colors, a whimsical sight.
With giggles as icing, we savor the fun,
Baking our way 'til the day is all done.

So pull up a chair, let's dig in with delight,
In the bakery of moments, each bite feels just right.
Together we feast, let our spirits take flight,
For in every sweet layer, there's joy in the bite!

Cake Crumbs and Cosmic Truths

In a world of frosting trails,
We chase down sugar dreams.
Each slice reveals a tale,
Of whipped cream and moonbeams.

Flour dust and giggling puns,
We whip the batter bold.
Life's lessons in sweet runs,
A recipe worth more than gold.

Sprinkles dance like stars at night,
Dancing on a velvet top.
With every bite, we take flight,
In a sugar-coated hop.

So grab your fork, join the fun,
In this oven of delight.
When life gives you a run,
Make cake, and hold on tight!

The Bakehouse of Belonging

In the warm embrace of yeast,
We find our crumbly home.
Knead together, an added feast,
With laughter, we're free to roam.

Cookies chime like laughter's sound,
Baking bonds grow strong.
In this haven we have found,
Life's playlist sings along.

The oven puffs with stories baked,
Of friendships forged in heat.
Each recipe, a path we take,
Beneath the floury sheet.

Taste the joy, feel the cheer,
As we frost our dreams anew.
In this bakehouse, hold what's dear,
Life's a treat shared among the crew.

Flavors of Life's Rich Tapestry

A swirl of jams and jellies bright,
Crafts a canvas wide.
Each flavor brings delight,
With berries on the side.

Chocolate drips with a wink,
As life's ups and downs collide.
In every bite, a chance to think,
About the tasty ride.

Carrot cake with laughs inside,
Surprises that astound.
In these layers, dreams abide,
A sweet life is unbound.

So let's bake our stories dear,
With whipped cream on the top.
In each slice, we hold what's near,
Together, never stop!

Mixing Bowls and Life's Lessons

In mixing bowls, we toss the dreams,
Some cinnamon, a sprinkle of cheer.
Life's messy, but that's how it seems,
With laughter rising, we persevere.

A dash of spice, a pinch of fun,
Twirling around like dough.
With every whisk, we're on the run,
Through valleys of flour we go.

Eggs crack like secrets shared,
In this batter of delight.
We add the joy, unprepared,
Mixing wrong feels so right.

Let's scoop the joy from every bowl,
Bake up some memories sweet.
With life's cookbook as our scroll,
Together, we'll rise to our feet!

Layers of Delight

In the oven, dreams arise,
Flour and sugar, a sweet surprise.
Frosting swirls, a colorful sight,
Life's a cake, take a big bite!

A cherry on top, what a thrill,
With every slice, I get my fill.
Sprinkles dance, like stars at night,
Sweetness makes everything right!

Cakes come in flavors, oh what a treat,
Chocolate, vanilla, can't be beat!
Each layer tells stories we weave,
In frosting and fun, we believe!

So grab a fork, let's celebrate,
With laughter and bites, it's never too late!
In the kitchen where joy takes flight,
Life's a dessert, shining so bright!

Enjoying Life in Full Flavors

Life's a buffet, a candyland spree,
Pie and pastries, why not just be?
Gummy bears giggle, they bounce and play,
Every sweet moment makes our day!

Chocolate rivers, ice cream lakes,
Whipped cream clouds, oh what fun it makes!
A cupcake castle in dreamy hues,
Let's toast with sodas, and dance in our shoes!

With sprinkles of laughter, joy fills the air,
Sugar and spice, no time for despair.
Let's savor the bites, both big and small,
Life is a banquet, feast for us all!

So let's slice up some joy, take a chance,
In this sugary life, we'll laugh and dance!
Every crumb and giggle, a tale to share,
In flavors and fun, we find our flair!

Whispers of Sweet Existence

In the mixing bowl, secrets swirl,
Baking magic begins to twirl.
Laughter bubbles like soda fizz,
Life's a cupcake, ah, what a whiz!

A sprinkle of joy, a dash of cheer,
Bite into happiness, hold it dear.
Whispers of chocolate, soft as a dream,
Life's sweetest moments, a frosted theme!

From cookies to pies, the flavors unite,
Each nibble dissolves all our fright.
With every bake, we learn and grow,
In the sweetness of life, let's steal the show!

So grab a plate, let's share and toast,
To desserts and laughter we love the most.
With sweet little whispers, life's joy ignites,
In the kitchen of dreams, our laughter takes flight!

Layers of Meaning in Every Bite

Slicing through layers, a tasty quest,
Each bite revealing what we love best.
Filling and frosting, oh what delight,
Life's a cake, let's munch through the night!

With a cherry on top, I make my plea,
Life's too short for bland history.
Pastries and giggles, a perfect fit,
In sugar-coated joy, we never quit!

So gather your friends, let's have a ball,
With pies and cupcakes, let's share it all.
In flavors so bold, we find our way,
Life's a delightful buffet every day!

Each layer a lesson, sweet or tart,
In frosting and fun, we share our heart.
So bake up some joy, let's not be shy,
For life's a sweet journey, oh my, oh my!

www.ingramcontent.com/pod-product-compliance
Lightning Source LLC
Chambersburg PA
CBHW072145200426
43209CB00051B/640